CW00663731

IN YOU

MELVYN MATTHEWS

Series editor Jeanne Hinton

Copyright © 1992 Hunt & Thorpe
Text © 1992 by Melvyn Matthews
Illustrations © 1992 by Len Munnik
Originally published by Hunt & Thorpe 1992

ISBN 1 85608 100 1

In Australia this book is published by:
Hunt & Thorpe Australia Pty Ltd.
9 Euston Street, Rydalmere NSW 2116

A CIP catalogue record for this book is available from
the British Library

Manufactured in the United Kingdom

CONTENTS

■ ACKNOWLEDGEMENTS

This book comes out of the experience of being asked to conduct quiet days and retreats at the Ammerdown Centre and elsewhere.

It would not have been possible without that experience for it forced me to think through what I really believe about praying and to formulate it in a way which people can understand and then, hopefully, put into practice. I would, therefore, like to thank all of the parishes and other groups who have asked me to talk with them about the spiritual life and to say that you have made this little book possible. It is dedicated to you all with thanksgiving.

Melvyn Matthews
Advent 1991

■ INTRODUCTION

This is a book which encourages ordinary Christian people to be more aware of the value of their inner life. It also encourages them to allow that inner life to express itself in their daily living. For too long now Christians have been afraid that opening themselves to this inner life is somehow either selfish or dangerous. This book is based on the belief that an awareness of our inner life will make us more aware of God and more sensitive to the needs of our neighbour and our world.

If you follow the chapters through and give particular attention to the exercises at the end of each section then, provided you have come with an honest and open heart and a genuine desire to come closer to God and trust his activity within you, you will find that your prayer life and your love for others will be transformed. Instead of continually worrying about whether you can pray and how and where you can pray, you will find your whole life becoming prayerful. You will find that you want to pray more more slowly and for longer periods of time. And that can only be good.

The Christian tradition has called this 'the contemplative life'. To bring this 'contemplative life' within the reach of ordinary people today I have called it 'Godspace'. It is the same thing. I hope that the different way of talking about it will release in you the same experience.

■ I

GOD'S SPACE IN YOU

I ONCE HAD AN architect as a member of my congregation. He became a good friend and I liked to visit him in his office and talk with him about his work. He would say that his job was to create spaces for people. He took his work with great seriousness, thinking carefully about how people used space and what sort of spaces made them happy or unhappy. He saw this work as having a religious dimension. He wanted to provide people with buildings which had a great sense of space. These were spaces which preserved or released their sense of wonder, their sense of beauty and proportion, spaces which gave them a sense of transcendence. He wanted to give people spaces to live in which never closed them down within themselves, spaces which prompted their sense of new and perhaps unknown possibilities, among them the possibility of God. He knew how the provision of the wrong spaces could diminish people and make them angry or afraid – unbelievers instead of believers.

The conversations I had with him taught me a great deal about the importance of space. Human beings need space in order to be fully human. They create spaces for themselves. A football stadium is a space. A house is a space. A cathedral is space. Even a road occupies a certain space and has a distinct influence upon us. Think of the effect of travelling along a narrow road and then coming into one of those broad high streets lined with houses which characterise English market towns such as Marlborough or Ludlow. Think how you are both liberated and settled in yourself as you make that transition. Spaces affect us more than we know. When they are right they help us enjoy life and celebrate our existence. When they are not there our spirit dies. They are vital to us.

We also need personal space. Personal space is not just physical space, the right size office, a big enough house or a wide high street. It involves physical space but is also something more than that. It is something less tangible but at least as vital. It is something to do with the amount of

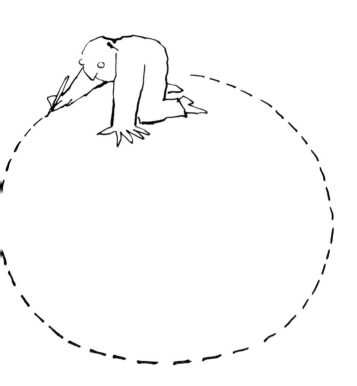

bodyspace around one, something to do with time, something to do with the pace of life, something to do with the ability to sense one's own being. People complain when they do not have 'enough space' and move jobs or locations in order to find more. I work in a residential centre where we welcome people from all walks of life and try to give them extra space in order to rediscover the true direction of their lives. So often people will come who are in what are known as the 'frontline' professions such as social work or the probation service or teaching. When they are asked what they are looking for they often say, simply, 'some space'.

This is one of the problems of modern living. Space, in whatever shape – whether physical, such as the spaces we live in, or personal, like the space we feel we need for our psyches – is difficult to find. Somehow modern living deprives us of the space we need. It is too quick or too crowded or too noisy or all of those things and more. We enter into this life with much energy and commitment and enjoy its benefits, but when we stop or visit other 'spaces' then we suddenly know what we have been missing.

Like my architect friend I do not think that this need for space is merely psychological. I believe that our desperate need for space is an indication of a greater and deeper need for God. We are all created with the capacity for knowing and loving God. We have within us space for God, what I call 'Godspace'. This 'Godspace' is innate but we have been living our lives without it. We do without it sometimes by conviction, but just as often by sheer neglect and the desire to fill our lives with something. What I want to do in these pages is to suggest ways in which our 'Godspace' can be restored to us. What follows has been written in the conviction that human beings have within them this innate sense of space which comes to them as gift both from the past and from God.

It is this sense of inner space which is God-given which has to be refound and lovingly preserved within the human life and within the human soul. When that happens we become more confident believers because we are less reliant upon getting out beliefs right and having to explain them to ourselves or others all the time. We also become happier, more settled people because we are strangely aware that God is with us. Discovery of and acceptance of our 'Godspace' sets us free to be, to believe and to be for others in a way which nothing else can do.

How this awareness can grow and be lovingly tended will be a central feature of this book. Without giving too much away it is important to say right at the outset that above all our 'Godspace' is known and owned by interior silence and prayer. And not only prayer but above all by the prayer of stillness, or the prayer of space which is normally called contemplation. Contemplation 'opens' our Godspace to us. This enables us to live as we are meant to live and love as we are meant to love. Without it we become victims of fashion and fancy, unable to be fully ourselves.

Living our Godspace, or being a contemplative person, is natural. It is not just for so-called 'religious' people. All of us are contemplatives. These pages help us to recover that natural sense and try to give some practical guidelines as to how that might be done and how it might be best done in a busy modern, fast moving world. In other words it tries to give some idea about living from one's Godspace, being contemplatives, without having to become a member of a religious order or even giving up normal ways of life. It is a book about preserving the capacity for contemplation, what some people have called our 'interior monasticism', within the confines of daily life.

■ EXERCISES FOR SECTION ONE

1. Find a quiet space. This can be anywhere from a church to a room in your home. It should be quiet and uncluttered. A walk in a city park or in the countryside is just as good as a room. Above all find somewhere where you sense the beauty and wonder of creation and can enter into yourself without feeling pressure or stress.

2. In this quiet space think about how space affects you. Think of all of your favourite 'spaces' and ask yourself why they please you. Don't restrict yourself to spaces inside buildings. Think of the country view or the city squares you like as well.

3. When you have finished or when you get home, make a list of these 'spaces'. Then spend half an hour drawing one of them on a large sheet of paper. Don't worry about whether you are a good artist. That is not the point. Just make an image of your favourite space so that you can know yourself better.

4. Spend ten minutes thanking God for the place that these 'spaces' have played in your life. Say over to yourself several times:

'The love of God is broad as beach
    and meadow,
Wide as the wind, and an eternal home.'

2

YOU ARE A CONTEMPLATIVE!

■ GOD'S PRESENCE IN THE SOUL

DAME JULIAN of Norwich, the English woman contemplative who lived and wrote her *Showings* in the fourteenth century, believed that the human soul can never be finally separated from God. This is because God dwells within it. She expounded this vision continuously, struggling all of her life with the way in which human beings, in spite of the indwelling of God, give themselves over to sin. For her human sin, however prevalent, never finally overcomes the glory of God's presence. She says,

> 'Greatly ought we to rejoice that God dwells in our soul; and more greatly ought we to rejoice that our soul dwells in God. Our soul is created to be God's dwelling place, and the dwelling of our soul is God, who is uncreated.'

This truth, which Dame Julian shares with the mystics of the church, is the source of contemplation. Contemplation is the attention of the soul to the presence of God. Contemplation arises from and derives its life from the reality of God's indwelling of the soul and the indwelling of the soul in God, and is the expression of that reality in prayer.

Dame Julian shares this understanding with St. Teresa of Avila, the Spanish mystic who lived nearly three hundred years later. Teresa likened the human person to a beautiful crystal castle in the centre of which God dwells. Meister Eckhardt, the German mystic, speaks of us as a mirror which reflects the sun so brightly that it actually is the sun. St. John of the Cross uses the image of a log in a fire which is so hot that it is both fire and log together. For them all this understanding of our basic unity with God was common ground and the source of immense delight and encouragement. Human beings can never, finally, be separated from God.

The insight of the Christian mystical tradition is that at the very deepest level of our beings we are not riddled with division and conflict.

Division and conflict result from our lack of relationship with the divine centre. Deep within the self there is a place of unity with God which in the end even sin cannot reach. There is an inner ground of our being which is the love of God. This inner ground is, however, hidden from us. We have alienated ourselves from it by fear. We have shut ourselves away from the very ground of our being by a combination of fear and the desire to achieve. Once we can re-unite ourselves with this inner ground then we will rediscover the reality of God's unceasing presence, and prayer will arise in us in a great fountain of love. Once we can put aside our fear then we will discover that 'Godspace' within, and rejoice in being naturally praying, contemplative people.

■ THE MODERN REACTION

The trouble is that this mystical talk sounds very specialised and a bit threatening to modern ears. Most of us can cope with the idea of praying, and, all being well, we do our bit. We pray in church. We might manage prayers on our own most days. We pray for things and thank God for things. But unity? God in the soul? Contemplation? It all sounds very well but we wonder whether it is quite our sort of thing. We're inclined to think that it is something for the specialists – people with a lot more time than we've got, monks and nuns, vicars even. Even then we're not too sure what use it might be. Praying 'for things' seems normal, useful, even if we're not too sure how it works, but contemplation does'nt sound very useful. It sounds a luxury sort of prayer.

These are the normal and immediate reactions which you will have when you hear about 'the unity of the soul with God' and 'contemplation'. Most people think contemplation is something which only those with time to spare can indulge in, and it appears to be a fairly useless sort of prayer because it *doesn't* 'do' very much, but it's probably harmless. It might well be helpful for certain people, but it is not the normal, everyday, run-of-the-mill sort of praying that most ordinary people get down to. We are not contemplatives!

But there is a whole world of difference between the way we think as modern, scientifically minded, people, and the way Dame Julian and the medieval mystics thought. Modern people think about prayer as a sort of action, a 'doing' which while spiritual in its nature still gets something done. Julian and the mystics seem to think that doing is not so important. Being is more important to them.

There are other differences between us and them such as the relative importance we place on things like acceptance and detachment. Modern people do not find those virtues very easy to practice. This 'world of difference' arises because in between us and the mystics lies the Enlightenment and the rise of rationalism. Because of the development of rational, scientific thought we know much more clearly than they did that if you think about things long enough you can actually change them. For example, you can actually destroy disease. The Black Death, which decimated the population of Europe in Julian's day, is no longer a scourge because we have thought and acted. Detachment, we would say, is not enough.

We find it extremely difficult to go back to pre-Enlightenment ways of thinking. It is almost impossible for us to value 'being' as more important than 'doing'. We are afraid, at a very profound level, that if we do we shall have to give up our reason and all that reason has achieved. So we find talk about contemplation difficult. Another thing is that, because of improvements in communications, we are much more aware that everybody in the world is involved with one another. We are aware of how this web of involvement is incomplete, and there is still a great deal of injustice, hunger, war and starvation. All of these things need changing. Christians have to work towards the establishment of the kingdom of God. Contemplation, we suspect, would at least delay all that by encouraging us to think about ourselves too much.

■ THE MYSTICS WERE LIKE US!

All of these fears, however, miss the point of what Dame Julian and the mystics were saying about God and about prayer. It also ignores the witness of their lives! None of them were inactive or lacked compassion for the world's ills. None of them were concerned for themselves before others, or found themselves unable to be rational and scientific – in so far as scientific knowledge went in those days. Teresa of Avila tramped across Spain founding convents and fighting the authorities on behalf of her sisters. Meister Eckhardt was an extremely busy university teacher and an administrator of the Dominican Order. Julian of Norwich was a source of pastoral care for all who went to her. They didn't make the distinctions between praying and doing, or praying and thinking that we have been worrying about. These are distinctions which the Enlightenment has left us. For them contemplation, 'being before God', or to use Julian's terminology, 'beseeching', was common property. It was not the exclusive possession of experts, monks and nuns, but a possibility for all of us. It was there as the foundation of our prayer and could be much more a part of it for most people than it was.

■ CONTEMPLATION IS OPENNESS TO GOD IN YOU

Dame Julian says that we will realise the full possibilities of this prayer once we know that its source is not in us but in God who is in us. In her *Showings* she tells us how the Lord revealed to her the central fact about prayer which is, 'I am the ground of your beseeching'. This is the source of prayer, and awareness of that basic reality opens the soul to God and brings unity and peace. She outlines all this in a beautiful section in the forty–third chapter of the *Showings*,

'But when our courteous Lord of his special grace shows himself to our soul, we have what we desire, and then for that time we do not see what more we should pray for, but all our intention and all our powers are wholly directed to contemplating him. As I see it, this is an exalted and imperceptible prayer; for the whole reason why we pray is to be united into the vision and contemplation of him to whom we pray, wonderfully rejoicing with reverent fear, and with so much sweetness and delight in him that we cannot pray at all except as he moves us at the time.'

■ CONTEMPLATION IS THE BASIC PRAYER

If you are open to the presence of God in the soul then you will know, as Julian knew, that contemplation is not a luxury, something you might do if you have time when all of the other modes of prayer have been properly fulfilled, but rather the necessity which undergirds all of your prayer and all of your life. Properly speaking it is the context for all other forms of prayer. It is the basic prayer without which all the others lose their integrity. It is the preparation for active and wilful forms of prayer, not an appendage after them.

Nor is contemplation a luxury in a world which needs justice and action for the poor. Contemplation is the context within which action for the poor properly takes place. Without it our action becomes mere theatre and politics, frothy action without direction or compassion or wisdom. Contemplation, people find, actually sets you free to be involved with the poor and the defenceless in a way which nothing else can. Because it is basically an expression of your inner freedom before God contemplation directly enables justice and peace. It sets you free from the principalities and powers which have prevented that justice and peace in the first place and so enables you to stand by the unfree without fear.

All this reverses much popular modern thinking about prayer and its relationship to the active life – thinking which suggests that human beings act first 'on principle', and then pray for guidance about their actions as they go along. The modern assumption is that human beings are action first, and 'being' second or last. This is something which certainly the mystics and now, at last, some recent writers about human psychology, would contest. We are now beginning to see that human action and praying are very complex. The primary mode of human living is not activity. Activity stems from a deeper level of consciousness which we can call, for want of a better word, 'being', and human beings need to put themselves in regular contact with this inner world of 'being' in order to be sane and mature. Without that regular contact they become superficial. Similarly, as far as praying is concerned, the primary mode of prayer is not 'asking for guidance', but something like 'being before God', and prayer which does not stem from 'being before God' is mere words.

■ CONTEMPLATION RELEASES THE TRUE SELF

The mystics also knew that 'being before God' releases energy rather than diminishes it. 'Being before God' does not put some sort of damper on your true self which is really meant to be out there doing things for the betterment of humankind, rather it enables you to know who you really are and what it is that this real self can do. It then sets you free to do it. What you are is a person who is part of God's being and his will. When you let yourself go into that being and will, then you will do what God is doing in the world and not what you think God is doing. Being before God enables activity of the right sort, it enables us to be true to who we really are. If we simply see prayer as 'praying for guidance' then the sort of God we are praying to is a long way off and we remain essentially unchanged. Contemplation sees us as being part of God and his constant redemptive activity in us and in the world.

If all of this is beginning to sound a little difficult let me illustrate it from my own experience. I once had a parishioner who found intercessory prayer difficult. She was a very devout Anglican whose father had been a priest and so she knew all of the arguments. She said intercession was illogical. Why should we ask God to give us anything if he knew what he was going to give us anyway. And so she told me that she was going to give it up. A little later she began to attend a Julian group, that is a silent prayer group devoted to a more contemplative form of prayer. In this group they would perhaps read a scripture passage or sit with a candle as a focus for meditation, but essentially they were silent before God. My parishioner friend went to it for a few months and then began to find that she *wanted* to ask God for things and that she could do so without difficulty. She found intercession pouring back into her life. Once she had reversed her priorities in prayer she found no problems with intercession. She no longer wanted to argue about it or think whether it could be done, she simply found it naturally taking its place in her life. I felt, talking to her about it, that this was because she had discovered the root of prayer in contemplation and being silent before God. Everything else was then added unto her.

■ EXERCISES FOR SECTION TWO

1. Find a quiet space once again. Take a piece of paper and divide each day of the week into hours. Work out, over an average week, how many hours of your time are devoted to *reasoning/deciding/doing* and how many to *being* or *delighting* in people or something beautiful.

2. Spend a good half hour alone, either at home or on a reasonably long walk and during that time ask yourself why this is the case. Ask yourself why you have succumbed to those pressures.

3. Decide to spend more time being rather than doing. In particular decide to pay attention to beauty of all kinds, whether this is beautiful music, art, the countryside or whatever.

Here are some suggestions:

• If you are involved in a number of projects, all of them very worth while, decide to give up one committee and spend the extra time practising prayer.

• Spend some time working out what is the most beautiful characteristic of your husband or wife, boyfriend or girlfriend. Decide to tell him or her what it is. Gradually do this with everybody you live and work with.

• Spend more time looking at trees – this is possible in the city as well as the countryside. Spend two minutes looking at a different tree each day. Buy a book about trees and find out more about them.

• Go to an art gallery nearby once a week.
Spend some time each visit in front of a
beautiful painting.

• Listen to Radio 3 on your car radio at least
once each time you go out, or go to a musical
concert more often.

• Find and keep a silent time each day of at least
half an hour. Spend nine tenths of the time
giving thanks.

5. Say the following prayer to yourself slowly
several times:

'O God, Giver of Life
Bearer of Pain
Maker of Love,
you are able to accept in us what we
cannot even acknowledge;
you are able to name in us what we
cannot bear to speak of;
you are able to hold in your memory what
we
have tried to forget;
you are able to hold out to us
the glory that we cannot conceive of.

Reconcile us through your cross
to all that we have rejected in our selves,
that we may find no part of your creation
to be alien or strange to us,
and that we ourselves may be made whole.
Through Jesus Christ, our lover and our
   friend.
Amen.'

(Janet Morley)

3

FINDING
YOUR INNER SPACE

EACH PERSON HAS within them a great deal of inner space. In order to be whole each of us has to recognise and welcome this inner space and accept it as the most wonderful gift. It is the source of life and unity and happiness. It is also the place of encounter with God. Here it is that we will come face to face with the Spirit who dwells within us.

■ FROM PRIVACY TO OPENNESS

What you must *not* do, if you want to pray aright, is to fence this space off, to privatise it and to regard it as exclusively your own. *It is not your 'private space'.* You call it private because you think it belongs to you and that it is absolutely your own. It appears to you to be the place where you are and where no one else can come. It is the place you think you can retreat to when things get rough and where you can

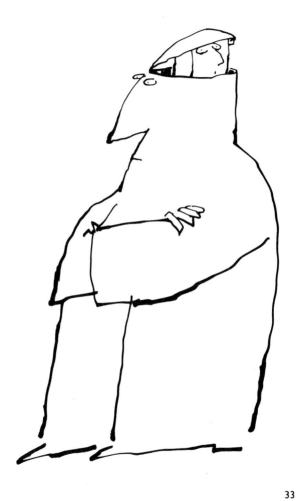

think your own thoughts. You think it is separate. Such an attitude is the death of prayer.

That this inner space is understood by many of us to be very private was illustrated for me once in a church discussion group where the leader asked people to share with each other something of their interior landscape. Share with us, she said, something of what is going on inside you. One person was very disturbed by this and refused point blank, saying her inner space was nobody else's business and even she didn't like what she had inside her so she was sure that it wasn't the sort of thing anybody else would like! This incident showed me that for most of us this interior world is not only private and separate, but often also felt to be somehow dark and difficult. It is somewhere that it is not always nice or easy to go because of all the difficult and perhaps evil things – feelings especially – that we might discover there. Like my parishioner we usually keep it well locked up and get on with our lives in the best possible way.

This is really a denial of the presence of God within us, a rejection of the glory of being human and whole. It is this fear of the inner space which prevents people from seeing that they are naturally contemplatives. Modern living reinforces this fear. We live on the surface of things. That is much easier and, it appears, more rewarding. But it is also very hollow. It is a way of living which can also affect our religious lives. They too are lived on the surface. If we are not very careful we pray and worship only using the active side of our lives. The result is that the habitual form of our prayers is an active, public, 'doing' sort of prayer. When we only live on the surface of our lives then our prayer is reduced to talking to God, who is just as busy and active and individualistic as we are. The only sort of prayer we can then possibly offer is the prayer for God – who is all powerful but very busy 'out there' – to intervene and do something about our situation! This turns God into an interventionist God who leaps into the breach only when things go wrong. But we know, somehow, that this is a caricature. God is not a whimsical, interventionist sort of God who suddenly does things; but we have made God like this not so much because we have not been taught properly but because we have not accepted our inner space with gladness and joy.

So if we carry on like that parishioner of mine – and I am sure that she was by no means unique – and refuse to enter our inner landscape with joy and expectation we shall be refusing the means to deep, satisfying prayer. We shall be denying our natural capacity for contemplation and so live unfulfilled and immature religious lives. We shall be left with mere words. The mystics point the way. Prayer and worship must come from deep within ourselves, from the centre of our 'centred' selves. This is really what Jesus meant when he said 'When you pray, go into your rooom and shut the door'. He did not mean that there should never be any such thing as corporate or public prayer. He simply meant that all prayer should stem from that interior space within where there is none other but '… your heavenly Father who sees in secret …'.

We might try to keep our private space private but in actual fact in so doing we are fighting a losing battle all of the time. It is a battle which cannot be won because we are fighting against the very nature of our being.

For in actual fact our so-called private space is not actually very private at all! It is not our own space alone. Happily and gloriously, thankfully and mercifully, it is inhabited by others. The recognition that our private space is not private is a source of mercy and forgiveness to the soul. Other people are there! Our parents are there, our brothers and sisters, those whom we love, those who have died and gone before us. Everybody is there within us who has contributed to our life. This is really nothing other than a source of great joy.

A twentieth century mystic, the American monk, Thomas Merton, talks about this experience of finding your Godspace as an entry into unity with everybody. He says that many people think that the contemplative life is a life of the 'alone with the alone'. Nothing, he says, could be further from the truth.

' ... one of the worst illusions in the life of contemplation would be to try to find God by barricading yourself inside your own soul ... The more I become identified with God, the more will I become identified with all

the others who are identified with Him ...
The more we are one with God the more we
are united weith one another; and the silence
of contemplation is deep, rich and endless
society, not only with God, but with men.'

■ GOD IS ALSO THERE!

But above all God is there! God has not left us
as isolated, private balloons, separate from each
other, divided in ourselves and ultimately
separate from his life. He dwells within us and is
present to us at all levels of our being. Roger
Schutz, the prior of the Taizé community once
wrote,

> '... you are never alone. Let yourself be
> plumbed to the depths, and you will realise
> that everyone is created for a presence. There
> in your heart of hearts, in that place where
> no two people are alike, Christ is waiting for
> you. And there the unexpected happens.'

There speaks the voice of the true
contemplative who has discovered that deep
within his deepest night the face of Christ

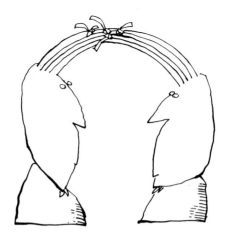

comes to him from beyond his deepest fears. This sense of the indwelling Christ informs and pervades every phrase of the prayers that Roger Schutz has composed. One of them begins,

'O Christ, in every creature you place first and forever a word: God's forgiveness and his confidence in us...'

Elsewhere he writes,

'When you are shrouded in what you cannot understand, when darkness gathers, his love is a flame. You need only fix your gaze on that

lamp burning in the darkness, till day begins
to dawn and the sun rises in your heart.'

And so, deep within ourselves we are united
with all things, all women and men and with
God. Modern living forces us to live apart from
all things, apart from each other and God.
Modern living forces upon us a dislocation. It
makes us live purely on the surface of things, far
from our inner truth, far from the Godspace
deep within us which is the contemplative
centre of our being. We are made, at the
beginning, to live from this centre. The mystics
call us back to this awareness. When we do we
become happy, contented, adjusted people. If
we return to the struggle of prayer, and
especially the struggle of contemplative prayer,
then we have begun within ourselves a process
of redemption and return. If we continue the
struggle then we will return our lives and the
life of our society to their natural, contemplative
source. We will begin the process of restoring
our prayer, our liturgy and, indeed, as we shall
see, our politics, to their natural and proper
beginning.

■ EXERCISES FOR SECTION THREE

1. Once again find a quiet space. Go for a walk or plan an afternoon at home on your own. If you are able, light a candle and sit before it quietly.

This time do a little self-exploration. Reflect upon your inner space and what it is like. Think about who is there and why. As each person comes to your inner eye remember them well and thank God for what they have given you in life. Go right back in your life until you come to your earliest memories of people.

2. If necessary take several walks or quiet times until you know your 'inner space' well and feel comfortable with it. If any time you become disturbed by bad memories find a trusted friend and share those memories with them. Do not become morose, always remember God forgives. Above all do not be afraid.

3. When you have finished find a large piece of paper and some felt tip pens. Spend an hour drawing your inner space. Don't worry about what it looks like, just make a picture of what you have found within yourself.

Whatever else is in your drawing include an empty circle to represent where you think God is in it all, i.e. around everything, or in the middle of everthing, in a corner, small/large or whatever.

Thank God for what you have found.

4. Memorise this prayer and say it to yourself frequently during this exercise:

'Give me a candle of the Spirit, O God,
as I go down into the deeps of my being.
Show me the hidden things, the creatures of
    my dreams,
the storehouse of forgotten memories and
    hurts.
Take me down to the spring of my life,
and tell me my nature and my name.
Give me freedom to grow,
so that I may become that self,
the seed of which you planted in me at my
    making.
Out of the deeps I cry to you, O God.'

(George Appleton, slightly adapted)

4

THE CONTEMPLATIVE'S GUIDEBOOK

A NY JOURNEY IS a journey into the unknown. A journey into 'inner space' is particularly frightening. You do not know what or who you are going to meet. The best travellers collect information about where they are going and look up all the maps beforehand, but are there any maps to your inner space? Aren't we all different? Has anybody been there before? Aren't we guaranteed a difficult time?

It might feel as if an exploration of inner space is a journey into the unknown, but that is certainly not the case. Our ancestors in the faith have all been there before and their journeys and their prayers are recorded for us. The Bible, both the Hebrew and the Christian Scriptures, are the maps of their journey and the record of their travels towards the face of God. We can take comfort that Abraham and Sarah, Rachel

It is that 'space' within which God makes himself known to his people. If you think about it, the wilderness is not just the wilderness of the Negeb south of Beersheba, but that space through which Moses led the people out of Egypt. It is where they were led by nothing more than a pillar of cloud by day and a column of fire by night. It is what the philosophers might call that existential space where the people came to know that they had to rely upon God alone in the darkness. He it was who led them there. Here they complained to Moses about their situation, asking to be allowed to return to Egypt where at least they had work and food, but they were led on and given manna to feed on and water from the rock to drink. 'The wilderness' is, effectively, the place

and Jacob and so many others from Moses through to Jesus and then on into the saints and martyrs of the church have all made the contemplative journey and have left us their stories as our guide. For the Bible is the contemplative's guidebook. Here are the records and here are the songs and prayers of those who set out into the darkness of faith. If your search for God frightens you then you have only to turn to the maps left here by previous explorers.

■ THE WILDERNESS

Think for a moment about 'The Wilderness'. The Hebrew Bible portrays God's people as coming to religious maturity in the 'space' of the wilderness. In the Bible 'the wilderness' is not so much an actual place as a religious place.

where the Hebrew people learn to trust God. They had to trust the word which God had spoken and placed in their hearts. They had to trust this word in the empty space of the desert and in the empty spaces of their hearts. If they were to do that, then, says the text 'You shall know that I am the Lord your God'.

We can begin to understand the deep religious significance of the happenings within the 'space' of the wilderness when we realise that this theme is not limited to the Book of Exodus but crops up throughout the Hebrew Bible. The events of the wilderness space are commemorated in a number of the Psalms, especially Psalms 105, 106 and 107. In Psalm 107 the wilderness is seen as an experience of being held in the hands of God's love and mercy and of being brought by God into a fulness of trust and love. In the prophet Hosea this experience is again seen as being at the heart of God's redemptive purposes. 'It was I who knew you in the wilderness, in the land of drought...' and 'Therefore, behold, I will allure her, and bring her gently into the wilderness, and speak tenderly to her...'.

And so the 'Godspace' of the wilderness is at the heart of the biblical message just as it is at the heart of the contemplative way. The contemplative knows that he has to abandon all of the familiar ways of knowing God and enter into the emptiness and the darkness in an act of pure trust. As he does this he is supported and encouraged by the wilderness experience of the people of Israel. The wilderness is often the theme of contemplative writers who see the need for modern man and women, preoccupied as they are with the Egypt of civilisation, to go out into the wilderness to recover their sense of the presence of God, who goes before them in the pillar of cloud and the column of fire. The Little Brothers of Jesus regularly spend time in 'the desert', whether this is literally the Sahara Desert or simply the empty quarter of a retreat house, in order to refind the God of their salvation.

■ THE PSALMS

We have already mentioned the Psalms. The fact is that this collection of hymns and poems is the primary source of contemplative wisdom in

the Hebrew Bible. Here, more than anywhere
else in the whole of the Scriptures, you will
come closest to that deep sense of the presence
of God which is at the heart of the experience
of those who have come to know their interior
unity with God, and the presence within them
of a 'Godspace'. Nowhere else in the Scriptures
do you come nearer to the very glory or
'presence' of the Lord. As you read them you
know that the Psalms both create and fill our
'Godspace' until your heart breaks for joy.
There is nothing the contemplative person
wants more than the opportunity to pray the
Psalms slowly and in silence, because they know
that in so doing they are brought before the face
of God in praise and in thanksgiving, in
supplication and in adoration, as by nothing
else.

In Psalm 27 we are brought before the face of
God and into the presence of God's beauty.

'The Lord is my light and salvation;
whom shall I fear?
The Lord is the stronghold of my life;
of whom shall I be afraid? ...

One thing have I asked of the Lord,
that will I seek after;
that I may dwell in the house of the Lord
all the days of my life,
to behold the beauty of the Lord,
and to inquire in his temple. ...

Thou hast said, 'Seek ye my face.'
My heart says to theee,
'Thy face, Lord, do I seek.'
Hide not thy face from me.'

All of the themes of this Psalm are
contemplative themes. The psalmist seeks the
face and beauty of God. He is ready to wait
until that face and that beauty shall be made
known. In Psalm 42 the same themes of
thirsting and longing appear.

'As a heart longs
for flowing streams,
so longs my soul
for thee, O God.
My soul thirsts for God,

for the living God.
When shall I come and behold
the face of God?'

And in Psalm 46 the theme of stillness before
God appears.

'Be still and know that I am God'.

Then another great contemplative theme
appears in the Psalms in the shape of the
creation, understood as that which carries God's
presence, is at one with him and which works
for his glory. This theme is present in a number
of the Psalms, but comes to a glorious climax in
Psalm 104. There the psalmist glories in the
riches of creation, and says,

'These all look to thee,
to give them their food in due season.
When thou givest to them,
they gather it up;
when thou openest thy hand,
they are filled with good things ...
When thou sendest forth thy Spirit,

they are created;
and thou renewest the face of the ground'

As one contemporary writer has said of this Psalm, 'Our poet is caught up in a contemplative view of the world, sensing its unity in the life-giving care of God.'

A contemplative view of things is quite central to the Hebrew Scriptures. John Eaton, the author of that quotation about Psalm 104, is quite sure that the Hebrew Bible must be placed side by side with the great contemplative books of the other world religious traditions. He says, 'When all is considered, it appears that the Old Testament has a great deal to contribute to the contemplative witness. This accords with the fact that so many contemplatives are found among the heirs of the Old Testament tradition: Jews, Christians and Muslims.'

■ THE NEW TESTAMENT

But what about the New Testament? Does that have a contemplative aspect to it? Surely, you will say, that is all about the action of God in Jesus and our action in response rather than our contemplation of him? But a little careful thought will show you how one-sided such a view really is. First of all the Gospels tell us that Jesus went into lonely places to pray. They tell you this quite often. He did so to such an extent that the disciples became concerned that he was neglecting the people. The Gospels also record a wilderness experience which they place at the beginning of Jesus' public ministry. Here Jesus, just like the people of Israel of old, learned to trust in God alone. Another experience, this time of transfiguration, is placed by the first three Gospels at a mid-point in Jesus' ministry. Again it is an experience of God in a lonely place. Before his crucifixion Jesus spends the night in prayer. The impression given by at least one of the evangelists, namely St. Mark, that Jesus is continually active and on the move, is hardly the whole truth. As far as we can tell Jesus' ministry was steeped in long periods of solitary prayer and he was clear on at least one occasion that miraculous activity could only happen because of prayer and fasting.

■ JESUS TALKS ABOUT SOLITUDE AND SIMPLICITY

The Gospels also tell you that the disciples asked him about prayer and that he taught them. Solitude and simplicity are the great themes of this teaching. 'Go into your room and shut the door', he says. 'Pray in secret to your heavenly Father who sees in secret.' When the disciples ask him to teach them a prayer he gives them the Our Father. The Our Father is a very short and simple prayer. Jesus gives us this prayer above all because he wants the prayer of his followers to derive from direct and immediate access to the presence of God. God is and God is present. He does not have to be invoked from a distance. His time is now. Moreover by giving them this short and simple prayer he is warning his followers against the overt and long prayers of those who pray in public and who wish to be seen praying in public. Jesus asks for prayer which does not 'heap up empty phrases'. We will not be heard, he says, simply because we have used lots of words. Prayer which uses many words is prayer which derives from our exterior self. Jesus is asking for prayer which comes from the deep centre of the self which is formed in the silence of our inner being and emerges from the true self rather than the false self. In this sense his teaching about prayer is deeply contemplative and has been the source of inspiration for contemplative Christians ever since.

Jesus' teaching as recorded in Matthew chapters 5-7, 'The Sermon on the Mount', is also deeply contemplative. It is here that his teaching about prayer occurs, but we also find here the authentic contemplative notes of absolute trust in God alone ('Do not lay up for yourselves treasures on earth...'); lack of anxiety about achievement ('Is not life more than food?') and attention to the beauty of the creation ('Consider the lilies of the field'). Above all Jesus asks us to seek the Kingdom before anything else. We are called to abandon ourselves to the love of God rather than the pursuit of wealth and success in this world. We are called to enter into the 'Godspace' of the Kingdom.

■ PAUL AND JOHN TALK ABOUT THE 'GODSPACE'

Nor should you think that the contemplative vision is lost in the complexities of theology when you come to the rest of the New Testament, the Johannine literature, Paul's letters and the other Epistles. John clearly talks about the unity not just between Jesus and God but also between the believer and Jesus; whereas Paul is sure that we are incorporated into Christ by baptism. Being 'in Christ' is what Christians are. For Paul the Christian life is derived from this basic unity in Christ.

The letters to the Ephesians and Colossians, which some scholars doubt were written by Paul, continue the same themes of the unity of all things in Christ. The cross of Christ has brought all things into unity, and 'we have died and our life is hid with Christ in God'. You cannot escape the reality of the Godspace within which we all live. It is almost as if any attempt to suppress it or to bury it under language or an intellectualist philosphy inevitably fails, and it has to burst through again and again.

The Bible then is the contemplative person's

guide and source book. It tells you where people have been and gives you some of the prayers they uttered. It shows you the people of Israel and then Jesus leading the way into the dark night of the cross and being transfigured into a living presence for us all. You can turn the pages of the Hebrew Bible and find all that is needed to inspire and direct the contemplative vision – the wilderness narratives, the psalms, the books of wisdom. The Gospels show Christ as calling us to live in unity with him and the Father in a life of attentiveness to the beauty of all things, simplicity and mercy. Paul and John too know of the same unity wrought by Christ in cross and resurrection, a unity which brings us to affirm that we are hidden in the Godspace with Christ the Lord.

■ EXERCISES FOR SECTION FOUR

1. Find your quiet space. This time take a Bible with you. If you are walking read the passage before you go and hold it in your mind's eye as you walk. If you are at home then sit quietly with a candle and the Bible open at the passages I shall give you.

2. Read through, at three different quiet times, the following passages:

a. The journey through the wilderness – Exodus 13:17—16.35

b. Psalm 27

c. Jesus' teaching on prayer – Matthew 6:5–13 and Mark 11:25

3. In each case make the words your own.

Imagine yourself to be with Moses and the children of Israel. Recall the times in your life when you had to step out into the wilderness.

Place your life into the hands of God as you say Psalm 27.

See how you can follow the teaching of Jesus about prayer more closely.

4. Pray this prayer at the end of your quiet time.

'O living God,
in our darkness you kindle a fire that never
    dies away.
By means of the spirit of praise,
you draw us out of ourselves.
To us, God's poor, you have entrusted a

mystery of hope.'
Within our human frailty
you have set a light that never disappears.
Even when we are not aware of it,
it is always there, ready to carry us onwards.

Yes, in our darkness you kindle a fire that
   never dies away.'

(Brother Roger, slightly adapted)

5

IT HAPPENS!

NOBODY SHOULD BE afraid of contemplation. It is not about special techniques. It is not just for the spiritual mountain climbers. It is not just for those with lots of time. It is not limited to a particular psychological or religious type of person. It is for all.

How then does it come about? Let me try and give some helpful advice, only remembering that this is not advice about techniques as if contemplative prayer was like mathematics or a foreign language which we have acquired from someone else. These are hints which, hopefully, will assist the release of something which is already there within us – something that is, as it were, waiting to happen.

■ WE NEED SOLITUDE

The first thing to say is something about our basic attitudes. We have to remember that solitude and silence are not alien or harmful to the human spirit. We are brought up in a culture which never allows us to be alone or silent for one minute. We have car radios, car telephones, portable television sets, portable computers, instant communication with anywhere in the world and so much more. None of these things are bad in themselves, but we risk losing our inner selves to their constant noise. They seduce us into thinking that we cannot do without them, and that if we do then we shall find ourselves without any identity. We have to remember, in a gentle way, that our identity is, that we are OK without, that we would be OK without anything. As Rilke said, we need to hear from ourselves more than we need letters from the postman!

We also live in a culture which assumes that maturity is indicated by being able to live with people. We naturally think that maturity is signified by living in common with an integrated and healthy set of personal relationships. People who want to be alone are often regarded as odd and those who need periods of solitude are thought to be those who 'cannot cope'. Fortunately, we are now beginning to see that much of this is very

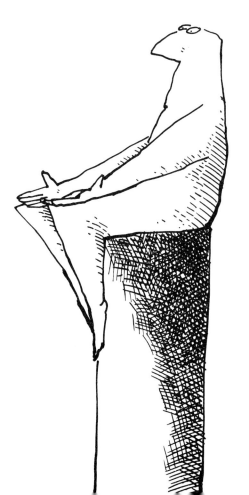

one-sided. A recent psychological study of the great figures of history shows just how much they valued and used solitude and silence. It also shows just how important silence and solitude are in the maturation process of the normal human being. The study marks a shift away from the psychology of the 1960's, which emphasised 'relationships' to the exclusion of all else. Nor, in one sense did we need the psychologists to point this out to us. We know just how much we need to be silent. We know we need to 'get away from it all'. Our retreat houses are overcrowded. Those deeply embroiled in public life, from politicians to media people and film stars, seek out monasteries where they can stay and be reminded of the realities their life-styles make them forget. The number of official solitaries in the church has increased dramatically over the last few years. People are seeking silence and solitude as never before. Recently in Sweden, that most secular of nations, a very successful television journalist gave up her career and now devotes herself to the running of a retreat house in the countryside outside Stockholm.

The first priority therefore is to remember that solitude and silence are not just natural, but actually necessary to the growth and maturity of the human spirit. As Anthony Storr says, 'Human beings easily become alienated from their own deepest needs and feelings... Learning, thinking, innovation and maintaining contact with one's own inner world are all facilitated by solitude.'

So here is my first hint: *do not be afraid to be alone*. When the opportunity comes for a few mements solitude, seize it with a glad heart.

- If you live in the countryside, go walking in the open fields and let your heart sing thanksgiving within you.

- If you live or work in a town or a city seek out quiet, silent places. Resist the temptation to spend your lunch hours in the pub or the restaurant. Resist the idea of going for a drink with friends after work. Find instead a silent space and enter into it. This may be a church or a park or a riverside bench. In any case find it. City churches offer space, some-times with lunchtime concerts or recitals. Art galleries offer space. Parks offer space.

- If you are a car driver resist the temptation to play your radio all the time. Turn it off or turn to music. Not loud, raucous music, but music which has plenty of space within it, music which comes from the interior of the composer or the performer. Allow that music to carry you for the day rather than the chattering commentators who love to fill spaces with words. If you drive a lot turn your car or your truck into a lay-by every now and again and give thanks for your life and the lives of those who love you.

- If you are with children at home then practice looking for those short, silent spaces in the busy day and make the most of them when they come. Don't always think, 'Ah, here's my chance to get on with this or that'. Make sure some of those moments are given to God, perhaps when the baby is asleep or when you are walking or driving to pick up the children from school. Stop saying to yourself, 'Life is one big rush!' It is only a rush if you let it be one and co-operate in the hurly-burly.

Moreover, whoever you are your 'silent

space' does not have to be a church or a cathedral or, indeed, anywhere special. It can be your bed, especially if you are frail or elderly. It can be a long stretch of beach or meadow where you can walk slowly with God. It can be your armchair. You just need to find it. Whoever you are look for these silent, empty spaces in your life and enter them whenever you can, for they mirror the 'Godspace' within you. Entering into them renews your contact with that Godspace and ensures that it stays active, secretly exercising its influence within the rest of your life.

Then, when you have found those empty spaces in your life and have entered into them unafraid, allowing them to greet you like long lost friends, what should you do? First of all **you should be silent**.

- Allow the busyness of life to drop away. Just be silent. Let the silence be a gift to you and for you. Feel in the silence that it is not empty, nor negative, nor even just neutral. It is a positive silence, one which is full of goodness, full of a silent presence. Open yourself to that silence and the presence that it contains. Allow that silence to join hands with the silence that your soul also contains. Don't speak, don't make prayers, don't feel you have to do anything, just become part of the silence of God which holds you and everything else.

■ THE PRAYER OF YOUR BODY

Then, in order to hear this silence more clearly, *let your body be part of your prayer*. This is really very important indeed. We are aware, somehow, that our bodies have got something to do with praying abut we have not given the matter any real thought. The consequence is that we are stuck with the more rigid body language that our surroundings or our upbringing give us – to disastrous effect. We need to feel our way into our bodies in prayer much more.

We do know about this really. When we go into a church or cathedral we usually find ourselves talking more quietly, walking more slowly. We might find time to sit for a while and give thanks for the beauty of the place.

When we attend a service we go in and kneel down and say some prayers, however short. We do feel we have to allow our bodies to express something. So the idea of using the body in prayer is not completely alien to us. The difficulty is that what limited body language we use in worship has become very stylised. My father, for example, who was a non-conformist, used to go into chapel, sit down and adopt what I call the 'eyeshade position'. As he prayed for a few moments he would put his left hand to his forehead as if shading his eyes from the sun and stare rigidly at the floor. He never looked at all relaxed or comfortable. Other people adopt the 'shampoo position', putting two hands on the top of their head as if they are about to wash their hair, again staring at the floor! Both of these positions and all of those like them force the body into a very closed stance, cramped in on itself, more inward looking than open to the life of God. They only make us uncomfortable and reduce prayer to a few quick thoughts – the quickness depending on how long we can hold the particular position we've adopted.

I can remember being much startled when I

first went to church in France and found that when people came into church they would often pray standing upright for a few minutes, quite without embarassment. This is certainly progress, for the whole body is then involved in an openness towards God. I would like to take all of this much further and make some concrete suggestions about using our bodies in prayer.

So when you have found your silent space and entered into the silence for a while, *make yourself comfortable*.

- Don't feel that you have to be in some rather rigid but stylised prayer position. If you are in your armchair or in your car sit comfortably and place your hands upon your lap, relaxed. If you are walking, walk with a regular stride. If you are in church then sit, rather than kneel.

Then hold up your head and straighten your back in a *stance of attentiveness*.

- First of all this is actually more comfortable. Slouching is not only bad for your body it is actually less comfortable than being upright and alert in a sitting position. More importantly, being upright is a stance which shows that you are attentive to God. You are then ready for whatever God has to say to you. In prayer, expectancy is all. It is also a position of confidence. We are first of all God's friends, not his slaves. We should be ready for the friendship.

So, keep your head up and focus your sight on a cross, an icon or a window. Shutting your eyes is not necessarily best. If you are walking, keep your head up.

Thirdly, **pay attention to your breathing**.
• Breathe in and out slowly, feeling the breath through your nostrils. Relax your whole body by deep regular breathing.

Then, after a little while, perhaps five minutes or more, you can simply **say, 'Lord, I am here'**, over in your mind and heart for several minutes.
• Resist the temptation to think that you ought to be doing any more or saying any more or thinking any more than that. You have placed yourself deliberately in the ongoing but ignored presence of God.

Passing the time correctly or getting the agenda right now becomes very much less important. Allow your inner eye to work, sensing God's presence.

You can see that none of this is 'an elitist technique'. It is not complicated. Most of it is common sense. It is simply a stilling of the external senses in a way which is common to a wide range of approaches to relaxation or therapy. The only difference is that here this 'stilling' is used to allow ourselves to be more conscious of the unceasing presence of God. The important thing is not to be either so alert that you are fixed in a rigid spasm of body and mind, nor so comfortable that you actually go to sleep! Prayer is an openness of the whole self, body and soul, to God. It therefore requires an openness of body language as well as an openness of soul. It is an attentiveness to God, a listening. It therefore requires a body position which expresses our readiness to hear. It is, by the way, perhaps this 'attentiveness' which distinguishes the person of faith from those who are simply using relaxation techniques as a form

of therapy. God continually speaks his word. Prayer is the means by which we make ourselves available to that word, and which allows that word to make us who we really are.

Some people find that this combination of comfort and attentiveness is best attained by using a prayer stool. These are simple wooden stools consisting of a seat about eighteen inches by four inches set upon legs. It is placed over the heels and so enables you to kneel down without either having to sit on your heels or to kneel upright, causing stress either way. It enables you to pray in a relaxed but alert and open position for a long time, especially if you also remove your shoes first. They are the modern version of the monk's misericord which you can see in abbeys and cathedrals. In fact the brothers at Taizé use them all the time and they are the standard furniture in their church for the community.

One last thing about using the body in prayer. What you do with your hands is also important. Holding them open upwards, as a sign of receiving, is one way. Others will hold the arms up with the hands open, particularly during the

Lord's Prayer. Some will stretch the hands into the air. But whatever one does the important thing is to allow the whole body to express the root of prayer which is readiness, attentiveness and openness towards God. Contemplation is passive in one sense, in that it is a stilling of the external self; but it does not involve a relinquishing of the inner eye and the inner expectancy. God is not the self. The Psalms remind us to wait for God and that is the essence.

There is one more hint to make before we move on to what can happen in the silent space. Many people find that once they have found their silent space and allowed their body to express their prayer then they need something to focus their attention. Some light a candle. Others light a candle before an icon of Christ or Our Lady. Others still place themselves before a simple bowl of water, thus reminding themselves of the stillness of God and of his clear but unseen presence. Some use the more traditional symbols, flowers or an open Bible or a crucifix. None of these are essential but they are helpful, because human beings are not pure spirits and need sacramental signs of the presence of God, who is pure spirit. You can make them at home. Every home has a candle or a bowl of water. Your 'Godspace' then arrives in your own front room. The important thing is to find fresh symbols rather than remain with symbols which keep us fixed in outmoded ways of thinking about God.

■ FROM WORDS TO SILENCE

But when you have found it and when you are silent within it and have opened your inner eye, what can you do? The important thing to remember is not to do too much, but here again, are one or two hints.

Recall a scriptural scene and imagine yourself there.

- This might be one of the miracles of Jesus or a scene from the Acts of the Apostles. Allow yourself to be part of that happening. Use all of your senses to smell the crowd, feel the heat, hear the cries and the dialogue. Imagine what it would be like to be there. Try to feel your way into the position of one of the disciples. Then listen to the words of Jesus.

Take these words into your mind and heart and open yourself to them. Don't rationalise about them. Take them on trust and hear them in your inner space as being spoken to you. Let them have an impact. Let them speak to your condition and open yourself to the way of being which they suggest. If you had been there, what would you have done as a result?

Or, you can be much more simple and dispense with imagining the scene and *hold in your inner ear a single saying of Jesus or one of the disciples*.

- This might be one of the Beatitudes, such as 'Blessed are those who weep, for they shall be comforted', especially when you are sad or bereaved; or 'Lord, I believe, help thou mine unbelief'. You should hold on to this phrase in your inner self for some time, offering it to God constantly. Instead of a Gospel phrase you might take a Psalm and simply say it, offering it to God as your prayer for that time. On another occasion you might reduce that Psalm to one of its verses and let that linger in you for a long time. A further alternative is the verse of a hymn or a chant, particularly one of the Taizé chants, which you can sing within yourself in praise or adoration, eventually allowing it to sit on the top of your inner eye while behind it you simply direct your inner gaze towards the God whom you adore.

- A favourite phrase for many people is 'Lord Jesus Christ, Son of the living God, have mercy upon me, a sinner'. This is known as 'The Jesus Prayer' and it can be kept in your Godspace for some time. Indeed some people carry it, or a prayer like it, with them all through the day, offering it up at every opportunity as a way of staying in touch with the divine presence and allowing that presence to be 'for' whatever is happening. You could do the same with a psalm verse or the line of a favourite hymn.

Then, in the end you might be able to *dispense with words altogether*.

- This is not unknown or impossible. Indeed there is probably much more wordless prayer going on than wordy prayer if the truth be known. Wordless prayer means standing before God with the mind in the heart offering to God what one mystic writer has called our 'naked intent'. In the end this naked intent is all that is required. Wordless prayer is the constant attention of the soul towards the God who loves us. It is not an act of concentration, although it involves the will. It is rather more like the search of the lover for the beloved. It is the offering of the self into the darkness of God. The great poems of St. John of the Cross describe it best.

'Without support, yet well supported,
Though in pitch-darkness, with no ray,
Entirely I am burned away.'

What I have described are a number of different models for a 'prayer of the heart' or contemplative prayer. I have begun with those that use more words or images and moved to those where words become redundant. It is worth remembering that when you pray each one of these models may well come into its own in one period of attentive, contemplative prayer. It may be that this is necessary, for it is difficult to slip into wordless or imageless prayer just like that. Maybe the use of a Gospel passage or a Psalm is needed as a way in to the utter silence which exists before God.

But in the end descriptions of contemplative prayer are very difficult to make. It is not something which is easily open to description as if it were something like a formal act of worship. This is because what we are talking about is the communication of the soul with Christ 'the courteous Lord' as Dame Julian calls him. It is a question of a relationship. perhaps the best way of thinking about it is how St. John of the Cross portrays it in his poems. For him the communication of the soul with God in prayer is similar to the way in which two lovers communicate. Sometimes they will use words – the ordinary words of everyday. Sometimes they will use gestures, gestures sometimes supported by words, sometimes not. Often, however, they will move into totally wordless communication, where each knows exactly what the other is saying, and that is so full of tenderness that words become incapable of carrying the meaning required. Sometimes only silence is the way that meaning can be conveyed. All of this is also true of our communication with God. The other merciful thing is that it is entirely your own. You have to pray as you can and not as you cannot. You have to find your own way of silent adora-tion. You can be shown where the path enters the wood, but in the end you have to make your own way with the unicorn leading you, glimpsed through the trees ahead every so often.

■ JOY IS THE LAST WORD

Contemplative prayer, or as it is perhaps best called, prayer of the heart, is really that prayer which takes over when words run out of power, just as friends or lovers have to have recourse to music or poetry or silence to convey the depth and extent of their relationship. Words fail us before the immensity of God. We know as much about God as we can see of an ocean, standing by the shore on a dark night with a candle in our hand. God is the immensity behind and within everything. We can only be full of wonder and awe before that immensity.

In the end the last word about contemplative prayer can only be joy. In the prayer of silence we are silent because we are full of the most heartbreaking joy, a heartbreaking joy which is focussed for us in the life and death of Jesus. We find we cannot use words without trivialising and betraying what we are doing. All we can do is stand before God with our hearts in our mouths and pour this joy of being into the silence of that immensity. That is, in itself, enough. We should not want to do more.

'Praise praises, Thanksgiving gives thanks.'

So, find a silent place or a silent moment. Enter into it. Give yourself to the silence, body and soul. Be there, in joy, before God. Even a moment is enough.

■ EXERCISES FOR SECTION FIVE

This whole section has been full of exercises. At the end of the book come back to it and go through them all carefully again.

Here is a prayer to help you through the

difficulties that will inevitably arise as you
venture into a life of contemplation.

'Like your disciples on the road to Emmaus,
we are so often incapable of seeing that you,
O Christ,
are our companion on the way.
But when our eyes are opened
we realise that you were speaking to us
even though perhaps we had forgotten you.
Then the sign of our trust in you is that, in
   our turn,
we try to love,
to forgive with you.
Independent of our doubts or even our faith,
O Christ,
you are always there:
your love burns in our heart of hearts.'

(Brother Roger)

■6

WHAT HAPPENS?

A T THE END of all of the thinking about prayer and all of the contemplative exercises which we have gone through in this little book there is one thing, a most important thing, which you must remember. Everybody who prays must remember this, but contemplatives more than anybody else. What you must remember is that the purpose of contemplation is not contemplation. The purpose of contemplation is the contemplative life. God wants contemplative lives, not simply people who go through the mechanics of contemplation.

If you have read through this little book and think, 'Ah, now I can enjoy a close relationship with God,' then think again and think carefully. Remember this: a close relationship with God cannot and does not exist in isolation from a close relationship with all things. A contemplative form of prayer brings you into a contemplative relationship not just with God but with everything that is. It enables you to reverence all that God has made.

Let me try to explain how this happens.

■ CONTEMPLATION AS A SOURCE OF GOODNESS

When you sink yourself into silent prayer all of what you are is lit by the fire of God's love. In that light you will be able to see just what it is that you need and just what it is that you do not need. Slowly but surely you will turn away from what is evil and move naturally towards what is good. What is good in you will then grow and what is unnecessary or evil will slowly but surely fall away. Contemplation enable you, because it is first of all a rootedness in God, to see things as they really are. You begin to be able to see things with the eyes of God.

Not only will you see the good, you will also begin to desire the good. This good was planted in you by God at your making. Contemplative prayer will kindle within you your innate and God-given desire for this good. This means that contemplation is, in the end, a moral force far greater than all of the exhortations to goodness which may be uttered by moralists from their pulpits. For it is true, as somebody said, that we cure our faults by desire more than by will.

All this can be summarised like this:

> **Contemplation will enable you to pay attention to what is good and to what is beautiful in and around you and to seek the good and the beauty of what you see.**

This should not be underestimated. Our world

needs people within it who are dedicated to the pursuit of beauty and goodness. We risk being overcome by ugliness as well as evil. If, in your prayer, you are constantly before the beauty and goodness of God then you will have an unquenchable source of beauty and goodness in your life. Your prayer will naturally lead you to eschew ugliness of living, ways of being which detract from the natural beauty of the created order. Moreover, evil ways of being – such as violence, cruelty, war, starvation, discrimination

of all kinds — will become anathema to you because you have within you a permanent presence of beauty and goodness as a check or judgement stone. You will know too that those people who are being degraded have a permanent presence of God within them which is being degraded. Violence, famine and cruelty then become blasphemies against the truth of what is within you and within all people. Constant awareness of the presence of God in contemplative prayer cannot but result in a deep and permanent reverence for the goodness and beauty of the self and of the selves that are around us.

An old Jewish tradition says that when a person walks along the street he or she is preceded by two angels who walk ahead calling, "Make way! Make way! Make way for the image of God!" If we are made in God's image and rediscover the presence of that image deep within us in contemplative prayer then we will also rediscover the presence of the two angels, so far hidden from our eyes by the pressures of modern life, going in front of ourselves but also in front of everybody else!

Contemplative prayer, then, lights up inside those who discover it a capacity for attention to beauty and goodness. This capacity, first and always directed to God, is also a capacity for seeing the beauty and the goodness there is in other people and in oneself. It is a moral force which prevents you from being too quick to blame others, and a moral force which prevents you from being too quick to see yourself as always wrong. It is a force which gives dignity to the human person.

■ CONTEMPLATION AND CREATION

But it also gives dignity to the created order. It enables you to see God in things because your heart is fixed on God in the first place. If your contemplative life does not release in you respect and care for the creation, then you need to think carefully about how you pray and why. God wants you to be someone who brings his love and respect into the world, not somebody who extracts themselves from the world in order to love and respect God without the world which he made and through which he is known. God asks you to see what he has made as being good in itself and having a beauty which men and women must not spoil. This beauty and giftedness is found in contemplation and must spill over into our daily living. This does not mean we should all live as vegetarians, or without petrol engines or the use of minerals or chemical fertilisers. But it *does* mean we should constantly ask ourselves, do I really need this? Some of us will come to the conclusion that we do not need quite so much. We will then be able to make at least one movement of protest against the spoiling of creation by not eating so much meat, by not using so much electricity, by not using up so many of the natural resources of the earth.

Contemplative people do find themselves to be, I believe, natural conservationists, natural lovers of nature, natural protectors of the countryside and its beauty. This stems from the discovery of the gifted beauty of things which contemplation brings; but it results in a protest, a prophetic word about the purpose for which the creation exists – the praise and glory of God. Nor should it come as any surprise that all of the great contemplatives of the twentieth century,

Thomas Merton and Brother Roger of Taizé, in particular, have been great lovers of nature and also great protestors against its misuse.

■ CONTEMPLATION, SILENCE AND SLOWNESS

Thirdly, contemplation brings a silence and a slowness into our lives. Modern life is characterised, as we are now well aware, by an increase in the number of words we use and hear and an increase in the speed with which we think we have to communicate these words to each other. We are pressurised by the way life is to speak without thinking and to judge situations too quickly. The contemplative person naturally comes to know that this is not necessary. This is because contemplation has rooted that person in the being of God rather than in the 'superficial life' of this world. Time is no longer of the essence and words become very precious. The contemplative person finds that he or she needs space in which to make a judgement. In that space he or she will hold the situation up to the gaze of God, will allow the divine presence to permeate it and show it up for what it really is. Within that space what is true and false will become more apparent. Speed destroys this capacity. Too many words make for a superficiality of judgement.

Silence before God inculcates a silence before the world. This silence is not a dumbness or a dumbfoundedness but a positive openness to the situation or person which faces us, a basic trust that what is is good and that the purposes of God are working for good for those who love God. A waiting upon God inculcates a waiting upon the world, a patience with the situation which faces us which derives from a proper

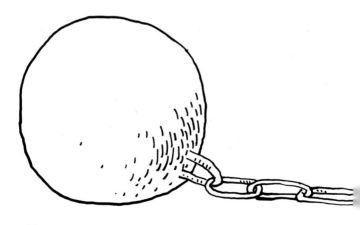

humility about our role in this situation. We are not the fulcrum of history or time. It is not our doing which will necessarily change things. God is at work bringing good out of evil. We cannot always see where God is at work and it is best to wait for a while before plunging rashly into things as if we were the prime mover in the situation which faces us.

This means that contemplatives will naturally be happier with a different pace or style to their lives, a pace which measures and waits, which listens and is silent because it is not compelled to act by the forces of immediacy and action. The

contemplative person is content to allow God to achieve things in them rather than constantly believing that all achievement is in our own hands. To use a theological tem for a moment this means that the contemplative is happy to be justified by grace, 'and that not of ourselves'.

■ PRAYING FOR RESULTS?

All of these things – silence and waiting, opennesss to the creation and attention to beauty and goodness – are all, however, the results of contemplation provided the contemplation of God is placed first. But we must not enter into prayer because we think it will do this or that for us. Prayer is above all a relationship of love and love just is. We cannot enter into it because we think that it will bring us certain benefits. We have to pray because we want to pray first and last and always. But if and when we do enter into prayer for its own sake, then, as it were by a hidden work, all of these other things – attention to goodness and beauty, care for the earth, stillness with others – will be added unto us.

■ CONTEMPLATION AND FREEDOM

Contemplative prayer is both a source and an expression of the freedom of God. What do I mean by that? What I mean is that in prayer you are uttering, as it were, a cry of defiance. You are defying the powers of this world. You are saying that not everything is determined. God is at work, God's purposes are present, although hidden, in the events of your life and of the world. You are saying that in the last resort you are free and exist within the freedom of God. Prayer is Freedomspace as well as Godspace. When you place yourself into the stream of prayer which arises in your life you are placing yourself and all things into the life and freedom of God.

Praying, therefore, sets you free. You are then free to grow, to move beyond the control of the forces that seem to dog your steps, to remove the invisible hands that grip you and keep you chained to your constant sins. You are also free, because of prayer, to stand with those who have no freedom and to defy the powers of the world that keep them there. That is why prayer is, in the end, a subversive action. It is subversive in the sense that it sets you free within. It therefore gives you the inner freedom to move in compassion to protect the weak and lift up the fallen. It links you with the love of God and places your will into God's will and your action into God's action. It is the source of delight and joy but also, because it is the source of delight and joy, the source of action against all that prevents and spoils delight and joy in the world.

■ '...STILL LONGING FOR LOVE'

We began this little book with some words of Julian of Norwich. Perhaps we can end with her too.

'And so we shall by his sweet grace in our own meek continual prayer come into him now in this life by many secret touchings of sweet spiritual sights and feelings, measured out to us as our simplicity may bear it. And this is done and will be done by the grace of the Holy Spirit, until the day that we die, still longing for love. And then we shall all come into our Lord, knowing ourselves clearly and wholly possessing God, and we shall all be endlessly hidden in God ... And there we shall see God face to face, familiarly and wholly.'

That should be enough.

■ BOOKS FOR THOSE
WHO WANT TO GO FURTHER

There are a lot of books available about prayer. Here are some about contemplation for those who want to take this adventure further.

BIBLE
John Eaton, *The Contemplative Face of Old Testament Wisdom* SCM Press 1989

JOURNALS
Henri Nouwen, *The Genesee Diary: Report from a Trappist Monastery* Doubleday 1976

Brother Roger of Taizé, *Struggle and Contemplation* Mowbray 1983

MINISTRY AND CONTEMPLATION
Henri Nouwen, *Clowning in Rome* Doubleday 1979

THOMAS MERTON
Contemplative Prayer Darton, Longman and Todd 1973

New Seeds of Contemplation Burns & Oates 1962

PSYCHOLOGY
Ann and Barry Ulanov *Primary Speech – A Psychology of Prayer* SCM Press 1985

VIDEO
The Seven Circles of Prayer Housetop Video